HUDSON

Written by JANICE WEAVER

Illustrated by DAVID CRAIG

TUNDRA BOOKS

Published in Canada by Tundra Books, a division of Random House of Canada Limited,
One Toronto Street, Suite 300, Toronto, Ontario M5C 2V6

Published in the United States by Tundra Books of Northern New York,
P.O. Box 1030, Plattsburgh, New York 12901

LIBRARY OF CONGRESS CONTROL NUMBER: 2009938456

LIBRARY AND ARCHIVES CANADA CATALOGUING IN PUBLICATION

Weaver, Janice
Hudson / Janice Weaver ; David Craig, illustrator.

Includes bibliographical references and index.
ISBN 978-0-88776-814-9

1. Hudson, Henry, d. 1611–Juvenile literature. 2. Canada–Discovery and exploration–British–Juvenile literature. 3. America–Discovery and exploration–British–Juvenile literature. 4. Explorers–Great Britain–Biography– Juvenile literature. 5. Explorers–Canada–Biography–Juvenile literature. I. Craig, David II. Title.

FC3211.1.H8W42 2009   j971.01'14092   C2009-905950-9

We acknowledge the financial support of the Government of Canada through the Canada Book Fund and that of the Government of Ontario through the Ontario Media Development Corporation's Ontario Book Initiative. We further acknowledge the support of the Canada Council for the Arts and the Ontario Arts Council for our publishing program.

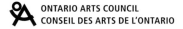

ONTARIO ARTS COUNCIL
CONSEIL DES ARTS DE L'ONTARIO

PRINTED AND BOUND IN CANADA

4 5 6   17 16 15 14 13

Contents

Now were all the poor men in the shallop, whose names are as follows: Henry Hudson, John Hudson, Arnold Ludlow, Syracke Fanner, Philip Staffe, Thomas Woodhouse, Adam Moore, Henry King, and Michael Butte.

ABACUK PRICKETT, 1611

Foreword

Unlike most early explorers, Henry Hudson discovered no new land or territory. On all four of his voyages, he surveyed waters and traveled coastlines that others had been to before him. He wasn't even able to find the passage to Asia he sought for so long. Some people think this made him a failure.

In fact, history has not been kind to Henry Hudson. When he's written about at all, he's usually depicted as a short-tempered man who played favorites with his crew and was driven by an overriding ambition that others couldn't match. But to sail through dangerous, ice-filled waters with only a small crew in a rickety old boat, he must also have been a man of rare courage and vision. And in pushing through the strait and into the great bay that both now bear his name, he helped draw the map of North America and, in doing so, advanced our understanding of the world.

GREENLAND

1610 Voyage – Discovery

HUDSON BAY

NORTH AMERICA

1609 Voyage – Half Moon

1607 Voyage – Hopewell

1608 Voyage – Hopewell

ICELAND

EUROPE

AFRICA

The Early Years

We know almost nothing about the explorer Henry Hudson apart from what happened to him between 1607, when he first set sail from England in search of a northern passage to Asia, and 1611, when he was cast adrift by his crew in the great Canadian bay that is named for him. Those four years are well documented in the journals kept by Hudson and his men, in his reports to his employers back home, and in the trial transcripts of those who mutinied against him. But the rest of his life is shrouded in mystery.

Although historians have uncovered very little information about Hudson's early years, they think he was most likely born in London in about 1570. We know that he had a wife named Katherine and three sons called John, Richard, and Oliver. We don't know anything about his parents, but it seems likely that his grandfather – also named Henry – was a founder of the Muscovy Company, a firm that traded goods between England and Russia, and that he was a man of great wealth and influence.

The younger Hudson was born at a time

when the world was undergoing tremendous changes. Less than a century had passed since Christopher Columbus sailed across the ocean blue to the New World. The Portuguese explorer Ferdinand Magellan had already attempted the first voyage right around the globe (called a circumnavigation), and Jacques Cartier had tried to establish a French colony at Hochelaga (now Montreal).

In England, Queen Elizabeth I was on the throne, struggling with conflicts between Protestants and Catholics, arguments over who would succeed her, uprisings and plots against her, and a prolonged war with Spain. At the same time, her nation was growing into an important seafaring power, and English ships and explorers had started traveling the world to find and develop new trade routes. Back home, people were becoming more prosperous, and many were learning to read and write, ushering in a golden age of art and culture.

Into this tumultuous and exciting time came Henry Hudson, a man driven – like so many others of his day – by a desire to stretch the limits of human knowledge.

Who Was HENRY HUDSON?

We know surprisingly little about Henry Hudson for a man who left his name on so much of the map of North America. We don't even know for sure what he looked like. All the portraits we have of him were made after his death by people who never knew him, so they may not look anything like him. In some, like the famous painting on page 38, he's shown as an old man with a long, grizzled beard. He was probably only about forty when he disappeared, however, so in the original illustrations for this book, he is portrayed as a much younger man, still in the prime of his life.

On the Hopewell

The first certain reference we have to Henry Hudson is from 1607, when he was hired by the Muscovy Company – his grandfather's firm – to take a ship and find a new sea route across the North Pole to Asia. No one would have put him in charge of such a dangerous venture if he'd lacked experience, so we can assume that he was already a skilled navigator and had been to sea many times before, possibly even as part of one of the explorer John Davis's three voyages to the Canadian Arctic in the late 1580s.

Hudson had apparently convinced the owners of the Muscovy Company that he would be able to sail right over the top of the world and down the other side to China. He knew that above the Arctic Circle, the summer sun shone for twenty-four hours a day, and his theory – commonly held at the time – was that the constant sunlight would melt the ice and make the land warmer the farther north he went. He believed there must be an ice-free corridor that would lead him right across the North Pole, and on May 1, 1607, he set off with ten crew members and his

The ART of NAVIGATION

Sailors in Henry Hudson's time had no easy method of figuring out exactly where they were. There was no reliable way of calculating longitude (from east to west) in those days, and the instruments for determining latitude (from north to south) were fairly unsophisticated. The most important tool in the navigator's arsenal was the astrolabe, which he used to measure the angle between the horizon and the North Star to establish latitude. An instrument called a nocturnal would help him calculate the time from the position of certain stars in the night sky, and a magnetic compass would show him which direction was north. Finally, the log was used to record a ship's estimated speed and the passage of time, and a navigator could then use this information to determine the distance traveled.

A seventeenth-century mariner's astrolabe

Close observation and careful calculations were critical to the success of any voyage. Even seemingly minor miscalculations could send a ship disastrously off course, causing it to miss its destination by miles or run aground on land that wasn't supposed to be there.

son John, then about sixteen years old, to find it.

Sailing into unknown waters was a hazardous undertaking that few men had the nerve to try. The handful of charts and maps that existed in Hudson's time were dangerously inaccurate, and the tools a sailor had to determine his location were complicated to use and imprecise. What's more, daily life aboard ship was extremely difficult. Men lived for months without fresh fruit or vegetables, surviving mostly on tasteless dry biscuits called hardtack, which were often infested with maggots and were so tough to bite into that they were nicknamed "molar breakers." The

The WHALING INDUSTRY

Hudson's report about a bay crowded with whales was welcome news to the owners of the Muscovy Company, who immediately began making plans to exploit this precious resource. In the 1600s, whale blubber (fat) was extremely valuable as a source of oil for lamps and wax for candles. And whalebone was used to make stiffeners for women's corsets and hoops for their skirts.

In 1611, the Muscovy Company sent its first whalers to Spitsbergen. The two ships took thirteen whales from the water, but both then met with disaster when one capsized and the other was driven ashore by ice. This was not enough to put the whalers off, however. Dutch, Spanish, and English ships were soon vying for whales at Spitsbergen, pulling them from the water as fast as their harpoons would fly. By the 1630s, as many as a thousand whaling ships were visiting Spitsbergen each year.

work was constant, especially for a small crew like Hudson's in the cold Arctic waters he sailed. Winds would send the boat pitching about, its every plank creaking and groaning and threatening to snap. Anything less than total vigilance could spell disaster. The men would shiver on open decks slick with ice, raising frozen sails with ropes that sliced right through the skin of their hands. High in the crow's nest, one sailor would keep watch for rocks or icebergs that could tear a hole in the ship's hull, all the time hoping for sight of land.

Hudson's ship, the *Hopewell*, was a decaying wooden barque (a three-masted sailing ship) built for short trips along the coasts of Europe, not an extended journey through icy seas. But it held together as Hudson and his men slowly made their way north of the Arctic Circle, past Greenland, to Spitsbergen, a remote Norwegian island very close to the North Pole.

At Spitsbergen, they found seals and walruses and a small bay teeming with whales. But they could find no passage through the ice. "I hoped to have a clear sea between the land and the ice," wrote Hudson in his journal, "and be able to circle north of this land." But every direction he turned, he found that his way was blocked.

After two and a half tedious months of searching, Hudson was forced to admit defeat. "There is no passage by this way," he wrote simply. Dejected, he turned his ship around and headed for home. But although he hadn't found a way through to Asia, he had sailed farther north than any man before him, reaching the northern tip of Spitsbergen, which sits about 580 miles (less than a thousand kilometers) from the North Pole. And he had established beyond any doubt that there was no passage to China across the top of the world.

North Again

If Hudson was discouraged by his lack of success, he didn't stay that way for long. He had barely set foot on dry land before he began asking the Muscovy Company to fund a second voyage. This time, he wanted to sail along the northern coast of Russia to find that elusive passage to Asia.

On April 22, 1608, barely eight months after he'd returned home, Hudson once again steered the *Hopewell* down the Thames River from London for parts unknown. On this journey, in addition to his son John, he had thirteen crew members – including a new master's mate named Robert Juet, who was soon to play a very important role in his captain's life.

Hudson's plan was to follow the coastlines of Norway and Russia to the remote island of Novaya Zemlya, in the Arctic Ocean. He believed he could work his way around or through this island to reach China on the other side. But this voyage seemed doomed from the start. Before they'd even left London, Hudson and Juet – who was described as a cruel man "filled with mean tempers" – had had a nasty confrontation that was just the

Of MARINERS and MERMAIDS

*Detail of a gold mosaic
floor tile, c. 1881*

The seventeenth-century world was growing more sophisticated, but many people still believed fantastic things that seem bizarre to us today. In Hudson's journal entry for June 15, 1608, he records matter-of-factly that his men have spotted a mermaid swimming alongside the ship. "She was close to the ship's side," he reports, "and looked earnestly at the men. . . . As they saw her, from the navel upward, her back and breasts were like a woman's . . . and she had long black hair hanging down behind. In her going down they saw her tail, which was like the tail of a porpoise, and speckled like a mackerel." What did the men really see? We will never know for sure.

first sign of trouble to come. Soon, the weather also seemed to be conspiring against Hudson. Even in the calmest seas, the *Hopewell* was dogged by thick fog that made progress impossible. Rougher seas tossed the ship about, its ropes and sails frozen solid. Then ice began to box the *Hopewell* in, and one morning the men awoke to "the fearful sight" of slabs of ice being driven down upon the ship and threatening to crush it. Hudson and his men sometimes spent entire days steering the *Hopewell* out of danger or fending off the ice with spare beams and oars.

But Hudson sailed on, trying first to pass Novaya Zemlya to the north. When ice made this impossible, he retreated south to look for a strait that his maps showed cutting right across the island. The sight of a large river with water "the colour of the sea" was encouraging, and Hudson sent Juet and several other crew members to explore it in a smaller boat. The men came back with stories of seeing deer and wild goose and even a piece of an old oar – proof that others had been there before them – but ultimately, they said, the river was too shallow to be navigated. Disappointed, Hudson declared himself "void of hope of a Northeast Passage."

Anyone else would have cut his losses and gone home, but Hudson decided instead that he would sail for what is now Canada and try to find a passage over North America. With most of his crew none the wiser, he turned his ship west and headed for the Atlantic Ocean.

Once again, things quickly began to go wrong. The *Hopewell* struggled through relentless rain and stormy weather, and the situation went from bad to worse when the crew finally realized that they weren't heading for home after all. Hudson's journal doesn't tell us exactly what happened, but we can assume from what he did record that the crew – perhaps led by the disagreeable Juet – threatened to mutiny unless he turned the ship around.

Hudson had little choice but to do as they asked – after all, he couldn't sail the ship without a crew – and he even covered up the mutineers' crime by insisting in his journal that he returned to England "without persuasion or force by any one or more of them." Pointing to the harsh realities of unfavorable winds and dwindling food supplies, he claimed that he had simply decided not to give in to "foolish rashness and wasted time."

And so, for the second time in as many years, Hudson sailed home having failed in his mission.

The SPICE RACE

Henry Hudson and explorers like him wanted to find a shorter, quicker route to the silks and especially the spices of the Far East. More valuable than gold, spices were used to add flavor to food, to preserve meat, and to treat all kinds of diseases. Bought for mere pennies in Indonesia, most spices could be sold for tens of thousands of times as much back in Europe. But there was still a high price to be paid for these riches. The sea routes to Asia took many months to complete, and one out of every three ships was lost along the way. Even those that made it safely back to port often limped in with just a fraction of the men who'd set sail, while disease, accidents, and even pirates and the occasional headhunter claimed the rest.

The Half Moon

With two failed journeys behind him, Henry Hudson lost the confidence of the Muscovy Company and found himself without a financial backer for his explorations. He sank into a deep depression, according to a friend, and could not be comforted. "It mattered not that his perseverance and industry had made England the richer by his maps of the North," his friend complained. "I told him he had created fame that would endure for all time, but he would not listen to me." Still, Hudson was not going to give up. He was convinced that a northern route to Asia existed, and he was determined to find it. All he needed was someone to sponsor him.

In November 1608, Hudson traveled to Amsterdam to meet with the directors of the Dutch East India Company. The company already controlled the spice trade – its ships reached Indonesia by sailing around the southern tip of Africa, called the Cape of Good Hope – but Hudson reasoned that a shorter, less expensive route would hold great appeal. He was right. In January 1609, the company's directors offered him a contract to search for a northeast passage on a Dutch ship, the *Half Moon*, under the Dutch flag.

Perhaps the Dutch had heard of Hudson's habit of sailing off course, for they gave him specific instructions to look for a passage around the north side of Novaya Zemlya – a route he'd already decided was impassable – and to "return immediately . . . with an account of everything whatsoever which shall happen . . . during the voyage." In case it wasn't clear that they wanted Hudson to go straight to Novaya Zemlya and back again, with no detours, they later added that he was to "think of discovering no other route or passage" except the one they'd asked him to explore.

Like the *Hopewell*, the *Half Moon* was no prize of a ship, but it could accommodate a slightly larger crew. Hudson chose somewhere between sixteen and twenty men – a mix of English and Dutch sailors – including the cantankerous Robert Juet and John Colman, who'd been first mate on the voyage to Spitsbergen. And once again, Hudson's son John was aboard.

Tensions between the two groups of sailors flared immediately. Juet pronounced the Dutch "an ugly lot," and Colman accused them of "think[ing] more highly of eating than of sailing." What was worse was that the Dutch sailors, used to the tropical heat of the East Indies, were poorly prepared for the icy waters and chilly temperatures north of the Arctic Circle. They complained bitterly about their situation and finally refused to go any farther.

It was mutiny again, but rather than punish his crew, Hudson seized upon the opportunity to abandon a voyage he'd never really wanted to make in the first place. He gave his men a choice: they could head west and search for the Northwest Passage near Baffin Island, or head south and look for a passage through North America near the British colony at Virginia. The men, not surprisingly, chose the warmer option. They set a course across the Atlantic, and in mid-July, having already spent about three and a half months at sea, finally arrived in the New World.

In what is now Maine, Hudson and his men met Native Americans for the first

time. Their initial encounters went well, but fear of these "savage" people eventually got the better of the *Half Moon*'s crew. One morning, Robert Juet led a party of men ashore to "drive the savages from their houses and [rob them], as they would have done to us." That fear seemed justified when, several weeks later, John Colman and four others were attacked by a group of Natives as they scouted a narrow river. Colman was shot through the throat by an arrow and died; the other men barely escaped with their lives.

These incidents aside, Hudson and his men had a tremendous time surveying the east coast from Maine to Virginia and back again. On September 3, they discovered the mouth of a large river and

GIOVANNI da VERRAZZANO

Henry Hudson is often regarded as the first European to explore the northeastern coast of America, but that honor really belongs to Giovanni da Verrazzano, an Italian navigator who sailed under the French flag.

Verrazzano first crossed to North America in 1524 to search for a sea route to the Pacific. Like Hudson almost a century later, he was convinced he would be able to sail right through the middle of the continent to Asia. He explored the coast from North Carolina to Newfoundland, sailing up the Hudson River, which he never named, to New York's Upper Bay. But – again like Hudson – he never found the passage he sought.

"My intention on this voyage was to reach Cathay [China] and the extreme eastern coast of Asia, but I did not expect to find such an obstacle of new land as I have found," Verrazzano wrote to the French king on his return. "[It] appears to be larger than our Europe, than Africa, and almost larger than Asia, if we estimate its size correctly."

thought they had stumbled on their long-sought passage at last. Slowly, Hudson steered his ship along this majestic waterway – the river that now bears his name – up a beautiful valley that, to him, was "as pleasant a land as one need tread upon." He followed the river as far as he could – anchoring one night off the northern tip of what is now Manhattan – until it was too shallow to go any farther.

Once again, Hudson and his men had to turn back. But they had found a habitable land rich in resources – a prize even more valuable than a passage to Asia. "We found good land for growing wheat and garden herbs," wrote Juet in his journal. "Upon it were many handsome oak, walnut, chestnut, yew, and an abundance of other trees of pleasing wood. In addition, there was much slate and other good stone for houses." Soon after Hudson's visit, the Dutch established several trading posts and settlements along what we today call the Hudson River Valley. And by the mid-1620s, they had founded a small town, called New

Amsterdam, on Manhattan Island. This settlement – now New York City – would become the most important Dutch foothold in the New World.

By the time Hudson docked the *Half Moon* at Dartmouth, in southern England, on November 7, 1609, he and his men had been away for seven and a half long months. They had survived storms, attacks by angry Natives, and yet another mutiny, but they had failed again to find a new passage to Asia. And still, Henry Hudson would not give up. Within a day of his arrival, he was writing to the directors of the Dutch East India Company to propose a search for a northwest passage over what is now Canada. He wanted to reprovision the *Half Moon* and set sail again as soon as the weather allowed, just four short months later.

The Dutch, however, had had enough of Henry Hudson. He had ignored their explicit instructions to travel only to Novaya Zemlya and back, and he had endangered their ship and their men for what appeared to them to be no real gain. They ordered him to return the *Half Moon* and its crew to Amsterdam as soon as possible. But before Hudson could make a move, the English government stepped in.

New Amsterdam in 1664, a little more than fifty years after Hudson was there

FIRST CONTACT

Fear of Native Americans was common among early European explorers and traders. In appearance, dress, and customs, the Natives were unlike any people the Europeans had seen before, and rumors of their "savage" behavior were widespread. It wasn't unusual for explorers to mistrust the Natives they met and sometimes even to act brutally toward them. In their minds, they were simply striking at these dangerous people before they had a chance to strike themselves.

But not all of Henry Hudson's encounters with Natives were as disastrous as the one that led to the death of John Colman. On several occasions, Hudson was able to trade knives, hatchets, and kettles for beaver skins and fox furs, and once he even went to a Native village as the guest of the chief. To honor him, the villagers prepared a great feast of maize (corn) and local game birds, then tried to persuade their guest to stay the night. "The Natives are a very good people," Hudson later wrote in his journal, "for when they saw that I would not remain, they supposed that I was afraid of their bows, and taking the arrows, they broke them in pieces and threw them into the fire."

Friendly relationships with Native Americans were essential to European efforts to explore and settle North America. In the 1500s Jacques Cartier was able to save his men from scurvy when the local Iroquois showed him how to make a tea rich in vitamin C, and later Samuel de Champlain depended on alliances with Native leaders to help his tiny settlement at Quebec survive. Natives showed British and French explorers new foods like corn, beans, and squash, and they led them to sources of fresh water and deposits of valuable minerals.

Most important, the Natives supplied the pelts needed to meet the demand for fur back in Europe. More than anything else, it was the fur trade that drove further exploration of North America, which led to the founding of frontier trading posts that, over time, grew into major cities like Montreal and Detroit.

To the New World

In December 1609, Henry Hudson and his men were charged with "voyaging to the detriment of [their] country" and brought before King James I to explain their actions. Although it was not unusual for explorers of the day to sail in the service of other countries, Hudson's trip to the New World had clearly displeased the king. The explorer was placed under house arrest and barred from ever setting sail under another country's flag again.

Hudson may have thought this was the end of his once distinguished career, but soon several wealthy and powerful men — including the king's own son, Prince Henry — came to his defense. They argued for Hudson's release and agreed to back him on another voyage to the New World, where he could at last search for the Northwest Passage.

On April 17, 1610, Hudson set sail from London with a crew of twenty-two men — including, once again, the disruptive Robert Juet and Hudson's son John. Their new ship, the *Discovery*, had barely reached the open sea when trouble began. Bad weather and poor winds slowed their progress and heightened tensions among the crew. Within sight of Iceland, Robert Juet was once again urging the crew to mutiny and threatening to turn the ship around.

Hudson was at least partly to blame for all the trouble on his ships. He was inconsistent in disciplining his men and mostly unable to control their behavior. Worse yet, he tended to play favorites. On the *Discovery*, for example, he sided with Henry Greene, a gambler of questionable character, when he picked a fight with the ship's surgeon and beat the man very badly. Because of incidents like that, Juet had little trouble stirring the crew's anger and turning the men against their captain.

Nevertheless, the *Discovery* sailed on. By the end of June, Hudson and his men had arrived at a strait that explorers of the time called the Furious Overfall because it was full of churning waters and dangerous currents, and was flanked by huge chunks of ice that could cut a ship in two. (We now call this the Hudson Strait.) Hudson, like many explorers, believed that this strait led into a body of water called the Sea of Anian, and that this sea in turn led to Asia.

Slowly, Hudson eased the *Discovery* through the rough waters of the Furious Overfall, past icebergs and soaring cliffs, until he reached what appeared to be a massive ice-free sea. He must have thought this was the Sea of Anian and the passage he'd sought for so long. Confident that he had at last achieved success, he sailed south into these waters – described by one crew member as a "labyrinth without end"– to find the way through to China.

For three months, the men sailed down the eastern coast of what they thought was the Sea of Anian but in fact was what we now call Hudson Bay. They searched in vain for a way out, meandering along the coast and arguing about which way to go. When Juet openly mocked Hudson's claim that the men would be in the Spice Islands by the new year, the captain had finally had enough. He called the crew together "to hear and bear witness to the abuse of some of the company," according to Thomas Woodhouse, a passenger aboard the ship. At this informal trial, it was revealed that Juet had urged his fellow crew members to keep loaded muskets and swords in their cabins, and that

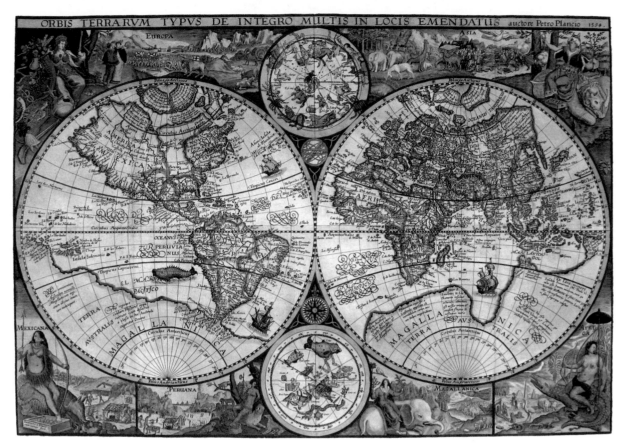

A 1584 map of the world by Peter Plancius, the official cartographer (mapmaker) for the Dutch East India Company

he had engaged in "so many and great abuses . . . that there was danger to have suffered them longer."

Hudson demoted Juet and cut his pay, but he must have realized that he could not go on without him and those who sympathized with him. Hudson needed his men to run his ship, and Juet's skills as a navigator were better even than his own. He offered to pardon them all if they promised to make no more trouble from that point forward. The damage had already been done, however, and Hudson was left with a dangerously divided crew.

And his problems were only to get worse. He wandered all over the bay, heading north, then south, then east, seemingly without any plan or purpose. He lost an anchor at one point and got the ship wedged in some rocks at another – none of which helped build the men's confidence in their captain. By the end

33

The GRAY KILLER

For men like Hudson and his crew, long months at sea with no access to fresh fruit and vegetables often led to scurvy, a horrendous disease also known as "the gray killer." Caused by a lack of vitamin C in the diet, scurvy at one time resulted in more deaths at sea than warfare, shipwrecks, and all other ailments combined. It was a terrible affliction that caused men's gums to bleed, their teeth to rot, and their skin to turn black and gangrenous. Without treatment, it led to a slow and painful death.

Scurvy wasn't eliminated from shipboard life until the late 1700s, when a daily ration of lemon or lime juice was added to the sailor's diet. But by then, the disease had claimed perhaps a million lives, either directly or as the result of ships that went down in storms or ran aground when their weakened crews had lost the ability to keep them from harm.

of October, the *Discovery* was trapped by ice, unable to turn around and head for home even if Hudson had agreed to do it.

The men had no choice but to drag their ship ashore and hunker down until spring, six long months away. Hudson ordered the ship's carpenter, Philip Staffe, to build them a shelter, but Staffe refused, arguing that the snow and frigid temperatures made the task impossible. Hudson, perhaps having had enough of his disobedient crew, exploded with rage. "He called for [Staffe] in his cabin to strike him," wrote one crew member, Abacuk Prickett, "calling him many foul names and threatening to hang him." Staffe gave in, but the small shack he managed to hammer together was all but useless against the bone-chilling Arctic cold.

As the days grew darker and the snow piled up around them, the men struggled just to survive. With no fresh fruit or vegetables to eat, they quickly began suffering from scurvy, which made their teeth fall out and their joints ache. Birds and fish became scarcer as the winter wore on, and soon the men were reduced to eating frogs and moss from the ground, which Prickett said tasted worse than rotten wood. The ship's gunner died of exposure and almost couldn't be buried because of the hard, frozen ground. And still, there were months to go until spring.

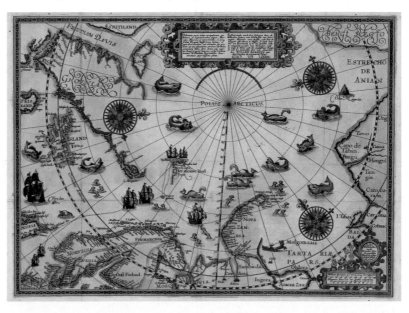

A 1598 Arctic map by the explorer William Barents

35

Mutiny!

In May—thirteen months after Hudson and his men had left England—the ice finally began to break up. Several crew members went out in the *Discovery's* shallop (a small boat) in search of fish with which to restock their dangerously low food supplies. One successful trip yielded hundreds of fish, but the men were never as lucky again. Starvation threatened, and the crew grew desperate.

One day, Hudson took the shallop himself and went to look for Natives who might have food to trade. In his absence, it didn't take long for the plotting to begin.

The men had had enough. They didn't share Hudson's desire to find a passage to China, and they didn't want to die in this icy wasteland so far from home. They decided that they were going to get the *Discovery* turned around, no matter what it took.

After several days, Hudson returned to his ship, having failed to find food or make contact with the local Inuit. Weeping, he brought out all the bread and cheese that was left aboard and divided it up among the men, promising to try to bring them home. They had less than two

The Last Voyage of
Henry Hudson
by *John Collier*, c. *1881*

weeks' worth of food left.

The *Discovery* did set sail again, but ice and calm seas soon stalled the ship's progress. By now, talk of mutiny was everywhere. When Hudson accused some of the men of hoarding food, and demanded that their sea chests be opened and searched, it was the final straw. "It was dark," wrote Abacuk Prickett, "and [the conspirators] were in readiness to put this evil deed into action."

At dawn on June 22, somewhere in the middle of James Bay, act they did. They grabbed Hudson as he emerged from his cabin and tied his hands behind his back, taking him and seven other crew members – including young John – prisoner. Prickett begged the mutineers "to remember themselves, and to do as they would be done unto." But Juet and the others were unmoved, and Henry Greene declared that he'd "rather be hanged at home than starved abroad." As Prickett watched helplessly, the captured men, some still in their nightclothes, were forced into the *Discovery*'s small shallop.

The mutineers hadn't planned to include Philip Staffe, the ship's carpenter, whose skills they knew would probably be needed on the journey home. But in a display of great courage and dignity, he insisted he be lowered into the tiny boat with his captain. "He said he would not stay with the ship unless he was forced to," wrote Prickett, and asked the mutineers to give him his sea chest and gun. Then he calmly took his place next to Hudson.

The *Discovery* sailed out of the ice with the shallop tied to its stern, but once it reached open water, the rope was cut. Hudson and his abandoned men, desperate not to be left behind, rowed frantically after the departing ship. But Juet and his crew simply raised the *Discovery*'s sails and rushed away. The nine castaways in the shallop were never seen again.

After Hudson

Only eight of the thirteen men left aboard the *Discovery* made it back to England alive. At the end of July, not much more than a month after they'd set Hudson adrift, four of the mutineers – including Henry Greene – were killed in a Native attack when they went ashore to try to reprovision the ship. Robert Juet fared no better. He and the remaining crew members ran so low on food that they were forced to eat bird bones and candle wax just to stay alive. Juet finally died of starvation sometime around the end of August, when the *Discovery* was at last almost in sight of Ireland.

It's a miracle that the ship made it back home at all. Toward the end, the men were so weakened by their lack of food that they could barely take the helm and probably steered the *Discovery* miles off course, adding precious days to a voyage that had already lasted twice as long as it was supposed to. According to Abacuk Prickett, the crew had stopped "car[ing] which end of the ship went forward." He wrote, "Some would just sit, watching the foresail or mainsail break free, the sheets either flying or broken, and not bother to

The transcript from the trial of the mutineers, 1618

Brought before the High Court of the Admiralty, the survivors pointed the finger of blame squarely at Juet and, especially, Greene, and all claimed they had known nothing about the mutiny until it was well under way. They argued that Hudson and the others had voluntarily left the *Discovery*. "They went willingly," declared Edward Wilson, the surgeon, while Prickett insisted that "no one was shot at or harmed in any way." One crewman, Bennet Matthew, even claimed that Hudson and the others had come back aboard ship for a time to warm up and to collect some clothes and other belongings.

But the court had a problem on its hands, for the remaining crew members had important knowledge about the search for the Northwest Passage, and one, Robert Bylot, had made heroic efforts to bring the *Discovery* safely back home. What's more, many people believed that in his failure to control his crew, Hudson had been at least partly the author of his own misfortune.

In the end, the court charged the men not with mutiny but with murder, "for feloniously pinioning and putting Henry

do anything about it or even call for help." When they sailed into Galway Bay, off the west coast of Ireland, they had to pay several men from another ship to pilot the *Discovery* the rest of the way home for them.

Once they were safely back ashore, the men set about the important work of blaming all the evil deeds that had taken place aboard ship on those who had not survived the journey home. With Juet, Greene, and the others gone, they had no shortage of people to accuse – and no reservations about doing the accusing, for mutiny was the most serious crime a sailor could commit.

Hudson, master of the *Discovery*, out of the same ship with eight more of his company into a shallop . . . without meat, drink, clothes, or other provision, whereby they died." All the survivors pleaded not guilty, arguing, among other things, that the looming threat of starvation justified their actions.

This last claim was hard to dispute – after all, the eight survivors had barely made it home alive, and Juet had not been so lucky. What would have happened if all twenty-three original crewmen had still been aboard ship? Maybe this thought weighed on the judges' minds too, for ultimately, they decided to free all the defendants, reasoning that it wasn't murder to cast a man adrift within sight of inhabited land.

We don't know for certain what happened to Henry Hudson and the other men who were forced into the shallop with him. In 1631, Thomas James, the English navigator for whom James Bay is named, described finding the ruins of a shelter that might have been built by Philip Staffe, the ship's carpenter. This may be proof that the men at least made it safely to shore.

England used Hudson's final voyage to lay claim to the rich fur-trading region around Hudson Bay, and this in turn led to the forming of the Hudson's Bay Company, in 1670, and eventually to the foundation of Canada itself.

The search for the Northwest Passage continued long after Hudson disappeared. The most famous expedition was Sir John Franklin's in the 1840s. When Franklin and his men failed to return, many other sailors went looking for them, and those voyages led them into areas that had yet to be explored, which allowed the rest of the Arctic to be mapped.

The Northwest Passage was not successfully navigated until 1906, almost three hundred years after Hudson, by the Norwegian explorer Roald Amundsen. Amundsen took three long years to make the journey, crossing from east to west, but he proved at last that there was indeed a sea route through North America to Asia, just as Hudson had always believed.

The remains of Henry Hudson have never been found.

Historic Sites & Monuments

The greatest, most enduring monuments to Henry Hudson are the places he explored that now bear his name – the Hudson River, the Hudson Strait, and of course, Hudson Bay.

Hudson River

The Hudson River – which Hudson explored during his third voyage, in 1609 – flows from the Adirondack Mountains, in northern New York, to New York City, where it empties into the Atlantic Ocean. Through the Erie Canal, it connects the Atlantic to the Great Lakes, making it one of America's most important channels for commercial shipping. The river and the canal together played a central role in opening new areas to trade and settlement, directly contributing to the growth and development of the United States.

Hudson Strait

The Hudson Strait lies along the north shore of Quebec, just south of Baffin Island, Nunavut. The strait connects the Atlantic Ocean to Hudson Bay, and thereby gives access to the interior of Canada. It was probably known to Norse explorers who sailed to North America in the 900s. But in his final voyage, in 1610, Henry Hudson became the first European to follow it all the way into the bay.

Hudson Bay

With a total area more than three times that of all the Great Lakes combined, Hudson Bay is one of the largest bays in the world. Because it provided access to the rich fur-trading areas in the Canadian interior, the bay played a critical role in the development of the country. Posts built along its shores and along the lakes and rivers that empty into it made inland exploration and trade with Native Canadians possible, which in turn led directly to the growth and settlement of Canada.

Reading about Hudson

The best way to learn about Henry Hudson is to read his own words and the words of those who knew him or traveled with him. Donald S. Johnson, a writer, mapmaker, and boatbuilder, collected Hudson's and Robert Juet's logs, as well as the journal of Abacuk Prickett, in a book called *Charting the Sea of Darkness: The Four Voyages of Henry Hudson* (Camden, ME: International Marine, 1993). To make the logs easier for a modern-day audience to understand, Johnson updated old-fashioned words and spellings, changed placenames to their contemporary equivalents, and converted distances from leagues to miles. It's essential reading for anyone interested in Henry Hudson.

Others have also collected Hudson's writings over the years, including the Reverend Samuel Purchas, who in 1625 published *Hakluytus Posthumus, or Purchas His Pilgrimes*, a four-volume work that is the main original source of Hudson documents. Purchas's book can be downloaded for free from the U.S. Library of Congress at rs6.loc.gov/intldl/drakehtml/rbdkhome.html. Also available online is *Henry Hudson the Navigator: The Original Documents in Which His Career Is Recorded*, by Georg M. Asher, and Thomas Janvier's *Henry Hudson: A Brief Statement of His Aims and Achievements*, which includes a record of the trial of the mutineers.

One final useful source of information about Henry Hudson and the other men who first explored the Canadian Arctic is the Dictionary of Canadian Biography. This too is available online, through Library and Archives Canada, at www.biographi.ca/index-e.html.

CREDITS & ACKNOWLEDGMENTS

Every effort has been made to trace the ownership of copyrighted materials contained in this book. Information that enables the publisher to correct any reference or credit line in future additions will be welcomed.

THE EARLY YEARS
Page 10: *Portrait of Henry Hudson.* Catalogue number 51246862 (RM) Henry Hudson. Stock Montage / Hulton Archive / Getty Images, Toronto, Ontario.

Page 11: *Elizabeth I.* Copyright © National Portrait Gallery, London, United Kingdom.

ON THE *HOPEWELL*
Page 14: *Champlain's astrolabe* by Foster, Harry. Copyright © Canadian Museum of Civilization, Gatineau, Quebec.

Page 16: *Eighteenth-Century Arctic Whaling.* Courtesy of the New Bedford Whaling Museum, New Bedford, Massachusetts.

NORTH AGAIN
Page 20: *Detail of a gold mosaic floor,* c. 1881 (mosaic) by Crane, Walter (1845-1915.) Copyright © Leighton House Museum, Kensington & Chelsea, London, United Kingdom/ The Bridgeman Art Library, New York, New York.

THE *HALF MOON*
Page 27: *New Amsterdam* by Vinckeboons, Joan. Courtesy of the National Archives, the Hague, The Netherlands.

TO THE NEW WORLD
Page 33: *Orbis Terrarum Typus de Integro Multis in Locis Emmendatus* by Petro Plancius, 1594. Courtesy of Hemispheres Antique Maps & Prints. www.betzmaps.com

Page 34: *Passengers and crew from Manila* by McGinnis, Robert E. Catalogue number 7100447 (RM) Artwork. National Geographic / Getty Images, Toronto, Ontario.

Page 35: Alexander E. MacDonald Canadiana Collection #248. Barentsz, Willem, ca. 1550–1597. Library and Archives Canada, HS/800/1598, NMC 21063.

MUTINY!
Page 38: *The Last Voyage of Henry Hudson* by Collier, The Hon. John, c. 1881. Copyright © Tate Images, London, United Kingdom, 2009.

AFTER HUDSON
Page 42: *Transcript of the Henry Hudson murder trial.* Copyright © The Mariners' Museum, Newport News, Virginia.

ACKNOWLEDGMENTS
First and foremost, I thank Gena Gorrell for her insightful suggestions, and her close and careful editing. The staff at Tundra Books greeted this project with enthusiasm and helped me in so many ways to get it done. Special thanks are owed to my friend and publisher, Kathy Lowinger, for her unending encouragement; to Lauren Bailey, for all her patient help behind the scenes; and to Scott Richardson, for the overall design and look of this beautiful book. Finally, I must thank David Craig, whose dedication and hard work brought the story of Henry Hudson to life in ways I couldn't even have imagined.

INDEX

Page numbers in italics refer to illustrations.